INDIANS
of the
WEST

Troll Associates

INDIANS of the WEST

by Rae Bains

Illustrated by George Guzzi

Troll Associates

Library of Congress Cataloging in Publication Data

Bains, Rae.
   Indians of the West.

   Summary: Describes the differing life styles of the
Indian tribes that lived in various parts of the West.
    1. Indians of North America—West (U.S.)—Juvenile
literature. [1. Indians of North America—West (U.S.)
2. West (U.S.)] I. Guzzi, George, ill. II. Title.
E78.W5B33   1984   978'.00497   84-2600
ISBN 0-8167-0134-2 (lib. bdg.)
ISBN 0-8167-0135-0 (pbk.)

The Indians of the western part of North America were as different as the land on which they lived. Some were rich and some were poor. Some were farmers, some were hunters, and others were gatherers. The traditions and lifestyles of each tribe were shaped by the land.

In the northwest—along the Pacific Coast —there were great forests with huge trees and lush green plants. The nearby ocean, rivers, and streams teemed with fish and shellfish, as well as water mammals. The northwest tribes, such as the Nootka, Kwakiutl, and Haida, had sturdy wooden homes, wooden boats, and a year-round supply of food. Of all the Indians of North America, they were among the richest.

To the east of these tribes—beyond the ridges of the Sierra Mountains—the land was bleak and dry. At one time, there had been lakes, but long before people settled there, the lakes had dried up. It was a poor land, and the Piute, Bannock, and Ute Indians who lived there were the poorest of all North American tribes.

In the dry regions of the southwest lived the Pueblo Indians. This region was mostly dry desert land, but there were underground streams that made farming possible. The Pueblo Indians grew fine crops of beans, squash, gourds, tobacco, and cotton. Corn, the mainstay of their diet, was grown in abundance, skillfully stored, and used in many ways. The Pueblo Indians led a comfortable, civilized way of life.

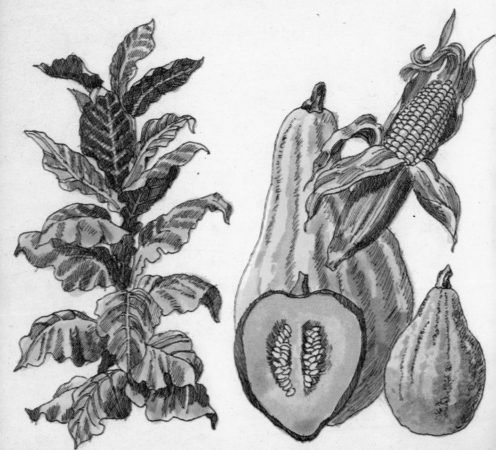

To the west—between the Sierras and the Pacific Ocean—lived the tribes sometimes called the California Indians. There were dozens of these tribes, all living in small villages, each speaking its own language.

These, then, were the Indians of the western portion of North America. Let's take a closer look at each of these four groups.

The Indians of the northwest—along the northern Pacific Coast—held great meetings called potlatches. A potlatch was given to celebrate a marriage, a birth in the family, a death, the inheritance of a chieftainship, or merely to show off wealth. The guest list for a potlatch was usually long. It included the richest and most notable people in the area, in addition to friends, relations, and neighbors.

The potlatch began with several days of feasting. Then, when everyone had enough, the host got up in front of his guests, praised himself, and bragged about his possessions. After that, the host gave away some of his possessions and those belonging to his family, and destroyed much of what he didn't give away.

One of the special articles given away or destroyed at a potlatch was a prized piece of copper. The copper was a thin sheet as long as three feet and engraved with different designs. The copper itself had no real value,

Attending a potlatch

but it stood for wealth and was used as a kind of money. A sheet of copper that belonged to important people was worth more than one owned by ordinary Indians.

Those who received gifts at a potlatch had to return the favor. They did so by holding their own potlatch and giving away twice as much as they had received.

The Indians of the northwest were able to be so wasteful because they had a bottomless source of wealth—the land on which they lived. The area yielded a constant supply of

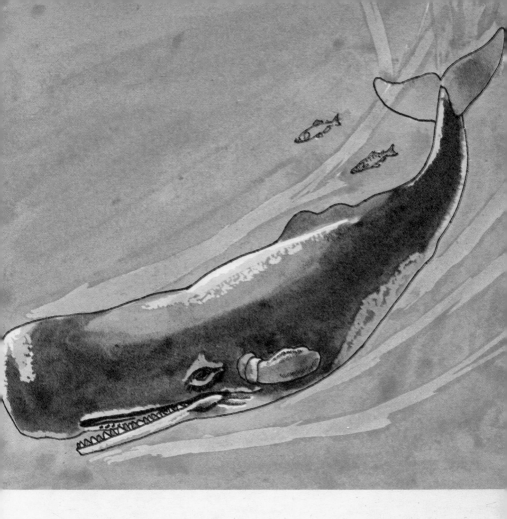

wood for their houses, canoes, tools, and religious objects. And the surrounding waters were filled with salmon, herring, clams, whales, seals, sea otters, and a host of other sea animals. The Indians' diet was mainly seafood, supplemented by berries and nuts.

The northwest Indians hunted land animals more for the hides than for the meat. They preferred fish and shellfish as food and were extremely skilled at fishing and whaling.

They used well-built cedar dugout canoes and a wide range of bone or wood fish-hooks. Their harpoons were armed with heads made of sharpened mussel shells and barbs of elk horn. The Indians fished for salmon by catching them in a basket-like trap, then killing them with a long, bone-headed wooden spear.

The tribes of the northwest lived in large, wooden plank houses. Each house was home for an entire "extended family." This included children, parents, grandparents, uncles, aunts, cousins, brothers, and sisters. In front of a Kwakiutl house always stood a tall wooden totem pole. It identified the clan, or family, that lived there. It also brought good luck and kept away evil spirits.

The Haida Indians also built totem poles
right into the front walls of their houses.
There was one at each front corner, and one
in the middle. The middle totem pole had a
hole near the bottom. This served as the
front door to the house.

In contrast to the wealthy northwestern Indians were the poor tribes to the east. There, the land was so poor and the climate was so dry that no crops would grow. The Piute, Bannock, and Ute Indians who lived there were forced to include in their diets such foods as jack rabbits, snakes, rats, grasshoppers, and crickets. But their main source of food was the roots of wild plants. They dug these roots out of the hard ground with sticks and stones. The other tribes of the American West looked down on these Indians and called them the "Diggers."

The Indians of the southwest were called the Pueblo Indians because of the homes they built. These homes were made of adobe, or hard, dry mud, and were called pueblos. *Pueblo* is a Spanish word that means "village."

The villages of the Pueblos were like large apartment buildings, with many rooms and terraces. The door to each room was a hole in the roof. To reach the roof from outside, an Indian would climb a wooden ladder.

To reach the roof from inside the house, an Indian climbed a notched pole that stood in the room. A Pueblo family usually occupied one or two rooms and used a third room for storing possessions.

Except for a few tribes, such as the Apache —who were very warlike—most of the Indians of the southwest were peaceful farmers. In fact, the name of one south-western tribe, the *Hopi*, means the "peaceful ones."

The Hopi and other Pueblo Indians raised corn and had more than fifty ways to cook it. They also grew cotton, which they wove into clothing and blankets. The only time they wore animal skins was when the weather turned cold.

Blanket weaving

Drilling holes in beads for jewelry

The Pueblo Indians were especially skilled at crafts. They created fine wicker baskets, clay pots, and jewelry made of shells, beads, and stones. The beautiful mineral called turquoise was one of their favorite materials for jewelry. The Pueblo Indians did not use silver until the Spanish taught them how to work with the shiny metal.

Religion played a great part in the lives of the southwestern tribes. The center of their religious ceremonies was the kiva. A kiva was a large, circular room built partly or completely underground. The door to the kiva was a square opening in the roof. It symbolized the hole through which the first people were said to have emerged from the earth.

The kiva was a place of prayer, meditation, and other religious practices. The religion of the southwestern Indians was a devotion to the spirits of the natural world— the sun, wind, and rain. Rain was the focus of Pueblo festivals, since rain meant life to the people of this hot, dry region.

To the west—along the southern coast of the Pacific Ocean—the land was fertile and easy to work. Strangely, only one tribe—the Yuma Indians—worked at farming. All the other California Indians lived off the rich land without making any effort to develop it into farms.

The chief food of the California Indians was acorns, which they collected and stored in their shells. This kept the acorns in good condition until they were needed.

In its natural state, an acorn is bitter to the taste. But the Indians found a way to get rid of the bitterness. They ground the acorns into small bits called meal. They soaked the meal in water until all the bitter acid, called tannin, was washed out. Then the Indians made the acorn meal into a kind of bread or cereal.

The California tribes built flimsy huts to live in, but they were superb basket weavers. Some of the finest examples of basketry were produced by the Pomo Indians of California's Sacramento Valley. Their baskets, decorated with colorful bird feathers, were so tightly woven that they could be used as leakproof water jugs. And the craftsmanship is so fine and delicate that it takes a magnifying glass to see the individual stitches of the baskets.

Among all the California tribes, religion was very important. It centered around visions, the spirit world, and death. These Indians held elaborate funerals and complicated ceremonies to show grief for the dead.

As in many tribes throughout North America, the California Indians never mentioned someone who was dead. It was considered an insult and very bad luck to do so.

After a person died, a California Indian family burned every possession of the deceased, including the home in which that person lived. And every year, on the anniversary of the death, relatives feasted and gave gifts to other members of the tribe.

Of all the Indians of North America, those who lived in these four large regions of the West were the last to be uprooted by the settlers. But eventually, the wagon trains, the discovery of gold in California, and the building of the transcontinental railroad brought an end to the traditional lifestyles of the Indians of the American West.